Grow Your Network, Grow Your Business
Your Guide to Intentional Prospecting

Joseph Novara

Thank You Susan!

Joe Novara

JOSEPH NOVARA

DEDICATION

This book is dedicated to my wife, Julie. Her inspiration and encouragement helped me to get this book across the finish line, and for that I am extremely grateful.
I love you!

JOSEPH NOVARA

CONTENTS

PART THREE: More Intentional Networking

PART FOUR: Mindset is an Inside Job

INTRODUCTION

Over ten years ago, during a lunch at the Carolina Coffee Shop in Chapel Hill, NC, my friend and mentor Earl Hadden told me, "It is the investment you put into your business relationships that will ultimately determine the level of success you experience in your business." I was already a strong believer in word of mouth marketing and leaning on my network to grow my business. However, Earl was talking about fine tuning my skills and enhancing those relationships. He was encouraging me to move beyond my *transactional mindset* and develop a *relationship mindset*.

At the time, we were at least one year into the 2008 recession. The printing company I had purchased in March of '08 was feeling the recession in a big way. We had lost almost fifty percent of our client base. Many of my clients had stopped doing any printing at all. Other clients began purchasing their printing on the internet because it was cheaper. They were willing to give up service and often quality for a much lower price point.

Based on that meeting with Earl, I realized I needed to focus my attention on the clients who were still with me and work hard at building up those relationships. And that is exactly what I did. I spent time with each of my clients. I learned everything I could about them, from birthdays to family member names to hobbies to favorite sports teams. Many of my clients became my friends. I developed very strong "know, like, and trust" relationships with them. To this day, I still have deep personal relationships with some of those clients.

In the end, for a variety of reasons, I closed my business on July 1, 2013. However, by the time I closed, our numbers were stronger than when I had purchased the business five years earlier. I had more clients than ever before. And we were earning more. This happened as a result of me growing my network and investing heavily in the relationships I was developing. My focus on growing my network led to increased business. And the increase in business led to increased revenue.

After closing the printing business, I decided to take a crack at a brand new business: public speaking and coaching. While it was new, it involved a lot of what I had learned after taking Earl's advice to heart. On July 3, 2013, I gave my first presentation in front of a large group of people at the Chapel Hill Chamber of Commerce. The topic was business networking, and it was well received. A new business was born!

A year or so after launching my new business I wrote and published my first book, titled "Intentional Networking: Your Guide to Word of Mouth Marketing Greatness." Like my first public talk, the book was well received. It even reached best seller status for a short time on Amazon. The stories, parables, and vignettes on networking were very personal, and I felt very accomplished after having published the book. However, over these past six years, I have learned and implemented many new strategies to grow my network and, thus, my business. Growing my network has taken many avenues. And each avenue has its own challenges, failures, and - best of all - victories.

That is how the title of this book was born. "Grow Your Network, Grow Your Business" is the necessary sequel to "Intentional Networking." While I believe very strongly in networking, there is far more to growing your business than networking alone. Don't be a one-trick pony, because sooner or later that trick won't draw the crowds any longer and you'll need other tricks. The same goes for developing exposure for your business: you must have multiple strategies.

In this book, I discuss many ways to build awareness of you, your business, and your brand. There are even some new chapters on networking that offer insights I have learned that were not included in "Intentional Networking." Be sure to complete the forms included throughout the book to help in the development of your network and relationships. At the back of the book, you will find a special URL you can use to download additional copies of the form for future use as well other goodies. Especially as you continue to grow your network and grow your business.

I hope you enjoy reading and learning from this book as much as I enjoyed writing it. I won't say that writing it was easy, but now that it's complete, it was well worth it. Growing a business through networking is my passion. I'm honored to share that passion with you.

JOSEPH NOVARA

PART ONE

Relationship Marketing

JOSEPH NOVARA

Chapter One

Kick Your Referral Relationships into Overdrive

In today's marketplace, we are told continually that in order to grow a business, most of our focus needs to be on the social media we are using. Whether it's Linkedin, Twitter, Instagram, Facebook, Youtube,, and the list goes on ad nauseum. Do I focus on one and perfect it or do I spread out a little over each platform? And, where do I find the time?

Maybe, just maybe, it's time to take a new look at one of the greatest marketing tools known to man throughout the centuries. The referral relationship.

I know there is someone reading this now that just screamed aloud, "DO YOU MEAN ACTUALLY SPEAK TO SOMEONE?!"

Yes, my friend, that is exactly what I mean. When we are hidden behind a computer screen, developing new business can become more difficult than developing new business through actual "in person" relationships. In most cases, human interaction outranks cyber interaction.

When you are referred to someone as a result of a "know, like and trust" relationship with someone else, your odds of winning this person over as a new client goes up significantly. While there will always be individuals who choose their financial advisor or CPA from an advertisement they stumbled across on a social media site, or late night TV, most people will not choose their most important advisors in such a callous way. Most often, they ask someone they "know, like and trust".

If you're on a tight budget, developing a relationship marketing system can also be much more cost effective than paying a high-priced expert to handle all of your social media needs. Don't be fooled however; there is a time investment involved here as well. But the rewards can and will be much greater as a result. Those rewards are completely up to you and the amount of time you are willing to invest.

Don't be one of those people that only calls on their referral sources when things are down. Your referral partners will catch on to that and begin to avoid your future phone calls. Like any good relationship, this relationship must be developed and nurtured. Not taken for granted.

Start off by being a giver. In the New Testament, Jesus said, "Give, and you will receive. Your gift will return to you in full - pressed down, shaken together to make room for more, running over, and poured into your lap. The amount you give will determine the amount you get back."

That is the law of reciprocity being ignited.

So, where do you begin? Start with the relationships you already have. In network marketing companies, new team members are encouraged to call everyone they know. Family, friends, co-workers, ex-lovers, priests, rabbis, shaman, etc. Although I do believe network marketing companies are on to something here, I don't believe you have to call everyone you know.

Be intentional about the people you contact. While it might be nice to catch up with Aunt Mary or with your friend James whom you haven't seen since the second grade, you will want to be deliberate about calling people that you can develop a referral partnership with.

If you're looking to connect with financial advisors, call your CPA. If you're looking to connect with CPA's, call your estate planning attorney. Or, maybe you're targeting home builders. Develop a referral relationship with a mortgage broker or a loan officer at a bank. Often times, the fastest route to the people we want to meet is through the people we already know.

This is where Linkedin can play a strong part. If there is a particular person you would like to meet, go to their page on Linkedin and see if you are a 2nd level connection to this person. If you are a 2nd level connection to the person you would like to meet, then you already have a 1st level connection on Linkedin with someone that has a 1st level connection with this individual.

You can now ask your 1st level connection to make an introduction for you through Linkedin. Make it easy for the person you are asking to make the connection by providing him with exactly the wording they should use to introduce you. Help others to help you.

Pick a target market and work it for all it's worth. Don't turn picking your target market into a ten point system, trying to figure out who is the best market to go after. You already know who your best clients are. Those are the markets you want to target. I always say, it is best to fish in a pond that is stocked with the kind of fish I like to eat opposed to a pond that is stocked with a lot of fish I can't or don't like to eat.

Talk to some of the folks you haven't spoken to in a while. Especially if you've done business with them before. Maybe it's time to have coffee or maybe just a short office visit. Ask them what you can do to help them? Then let them know who it is you're looking to meet these days. It's been awhile since you've spoken to this person, so your target may have changed, or they probably have forgotten. Be specific when sharing who your target client is. And, be sure to ask specifically who they are looking to be connected to these days.

We also want to develop new referral relationships. These relationships will come as a result of some of the referrals we receive and from the networking events we attend. I want to be clear here. If you focus on a specific niche, do not spend your time attending the local networking mixers or leads groups. That brings us back to the two ponds. Go to where the fish (your potential clients and referral sources) are plentiful. This is an opportunity for you to focus on the associations and other organizations affiliated with your target market.

Networking mixers, Chamber of Commerce events and other leads groups are not bad. As a matter of fact, they can be quite good. If you're business is one that is not focused on one specific market, ie. a local real estate sales agent, distributor for health supplements or an accountant, then a networking mixer may serve you well. They were great for me when I first started my coaching practice.

It is important that we are intentional about the networking we do. Networking takes time and time is money. Unless you're a bored socialite, don't waste your time at business events that are going to get you anything but new business.

While I am a big believer in face to face business networking, social media is still very important for you and the growth of your business. However, I suggest you allow it to be <u>a part</u> of your marketing platform, not the main focus. Too many people these days are putting all their focus, time and attention into social media activities and then wonder why they are not developing new business at a rate they would like.

I am not a social media expert and I do know what has worked well for me. My preference has been to utilize the big four. I have goals and strategies for each of the platforms I use.

I use Facebook heavily for announcing my local speaking events and group coaching dates. It is great to announce events and to celebrate achievements. People like to see their friends and peers reach new levels of growth. Personally, I have not had great success with the paid ads, however, others have. I suggest if you are going to pay for an ad, invest very little money and run a couple of tests first. Record your results and decide if it is worth it to invest more.

As for Twitter, I don't tweet often enough to say it has benefited me, however, I do use it at least a few times a week. It is usually to make announcements or to retweet something of value I found from someone else. I also like to tweet the URL's for articles I enjoyed if there is an option to do so at the end of the article.

I really enjoy using Instagram and have been building a following on it. I feel confident to say that I believe it is highly important in today's marketplace. Why do I say that? Well, because Facebook paid $1 billion for it and it is currently worth almost 50 times what they originally paid for it. At the time of writing this book, I post on Instagram almost daily and I'm building a healthy audience in my target market. Maybe in my next book I can share with you all the successes I have had as a result of my Instagram activity. Thanks for the encouragement Gary V.

The social media platform I get the most use out of is LinkedIn. I have found LinkedIn to be a great prospecting tool. I have developed wonderful prospecting lists using LinkedIn. I have also created new business relationships that started from LinkedIn connections. LinkedIn is an extremely powerful tool that many professionals are not using effectively. While it appears that LinkedIn is moving closer to wanting to be paid for many of the now free features, there are still many available on the free platform that you can use to build a great database to prospect from.

While I do believe social media is important, I feel much stronger about the power of human interaction. Face to face. Belly to belly. That's how we develop our referral relationships. If you're uncomfortable with speaking to people, join a local Toastmasters chapter. You can learn some incredible skills on interacting with others in Toastmasters. Another option is to read my book, "Intentional Networking," which teaches fellow introverts and shy people how to overcome the overwhelm many people feel around networking.

Identify who your go to professional or potential referral source is for each of the following professions in the list below. If you can't fill in a specific name now, look for opportunities as Your Grow Your Network.

Business Type	Referral Source/Partner
CPA	_____
Real Estate Agent	_____
Chiropractor	_____
Business Coach	_____
Home Security Expert	_____
Carpet Cleaner	_____
Home Builder	_____
Credit Card Proc.	_____
Life Insurance Rep	_____
Home Inspector	_____
Financial Advisor	_____
Printer	_____
Web Designer	_____
Estate Planning Attny	_____
Interior Decorator	_____
Promo Item Distributor	_____
Electrician	_____
IT Company	_____
Dentist	_____
Personal Injury Attny	_____
Senior Assistance	_____
Damage/Restoration	_____

Notes

_____

_____

_____

_____

_____

_____

_____

_____

_____

_____

_____

_____

_____

_____

_____

_____

_____

_____

Chapter Two

Referral Marketing –
Let's Keep it Simple

Referral marketing may possibly be the easiest form of marketing. At the same time, referral marketing is really difficult too. An effective referral Marketing System involves many variables. However, I will share with you some ways to use referral marketing to increase your sales quickly and inexpensively, without spinning your wheels.

Let's begin with language. The specific words we use to tell others about ourselves and our business are critical. Equally important are the words that others use in telling their Network about us and our business. First, there needs to be a reason somebody is going to buy from us. That may be a pain point, a problem, or just a desire. Whatever it is, we must clearly express it. And we must also clearly state that we can fill that need.

Next, we must identify who our ideal client is. If I don't know who my ideal client is, that means I have not identified a specific pain, problem or need. In that case, my marketing is like throwing a dart at a dartboard while blindfolded – very rarely will I hit the bullseye. Heck, it's hard enough to hit the bullseye without a blindfold!

Once I have identified my ideal target client and their need, next I will develop the precise language for sharing my offering. We want our language to clearly communicate three things to referral partners, referral sources, and prospects. First is the PROBLEM. Second is our SOLUTION to the PROBLEM. Third, we must share two to three BENEFITS they will receive from our SOLUTION. The BENEFITS are the most important of the three. Make it easy for folks who are referring you to share those BENEFITS just as clearly as you can. Here is an example of my three elements:

PROBLEM: "Many professionals want to grow their business by referral but they've never learned a system for doing so. As a result, they spin their wheels, waste a lot of precious time, and feel frustrated."

SOLUTION: "My coaching program, The Referral Marketing Success System, helps professionals create and organize an effective referral marketing process."

BENEFITS: "Then they're able to organize their referral process, receive more referrals, and in turn, make more money."

I can use any one of those three elements when somebody asks me what I do. For example, I can just start off with the BENEFITS. If asked, "So what do you do, Joe?" I can easily answer, "I teach busy professionals how to organize their referral process, receive more referrals, and in turn, make more money." That would certainly sound intriguing to me if I wasn't already doing it.

The two main take-aways I want you to get here are: (a) be clear on who your ideal target client is, and (b) make it easy for others to share what it is you do and the benefits they will get from working with you. This system produces incredible results for me and has been a game changer for many of my coaching clients. Implement it in the language you use, and it could very well be a game changer for you as well.

Notes

Chapter Three

Building Client Relationships That Last

It's no secret that generally the most valuable and profitable clients are those with whom you develop a close relationship over time. But how do you develop that client relationship?

When I make a new personal friendship, it often starts by meeting them at a party, at church, at the gym, at a business event or at any other number of daily life events. That friendship is then built over time, based on getting to know each other, finding common interests that create likeability, and developing trust between each other.

Building relationships with a client is very similar to building personal relationships. After two companies or two parties agree to do business, if you are intentional, you can create a level of comfort, which will allow for the relationship to blossom. The relationship won't necessarily grow into the type where the businesses or their families get together at the holidays (although sometimes that happens). But it certainly can generate a level of care and long-term respect for each other – which will pay off in the long run.

Sales master Harvey Mackay has a list of 66 details he requires his salespeople to collect about clients over time. He not only wants his salespeople to learn information required to do business; he wants them to learn personal information about them as well. Personal details such as birthdays, whether they are married, whether they have children, and even the names of their spouse and children.

Over the course of the relationship, this information will be used to have a continuing conversation, and in turn to develop trust and long-lasting likeability. I highly encourage you to find online and download a copy of the "Mackay 66" online. Using this tool will be invaluable to your sales efforts.

My father was incredibly well liked in the printing industry, both in the U.S. and around the world. He was in the industry for over 25 years and developed relationships with hundreds of people. When he passed away, the owner of the company he worked for rented three limousines for the funeral. Not only did his coworkers want to attend his funeral, many of the clients and vendors my father had worked with for years also wanted to pay their respects. He was a man of great integrity. He had an ability to connect with people and make them feel important and cared for, no matter what their position was. It became apparent on the day of his funeral!

One of the platforms Bob Burg, author of the great books, "Endless Referrals" and "The Go Giver", built his speaking and writing career on is the principal that people do business with people they know, like, and trust. Show your client you honestly care about them. Always have the mindset of, "What can I do for you?" and display that behavior proudly. Get to know your clients well. Help them in any way you can. And make them feel important. In time, they will want to see you, spend time with you, and continue to buy from you.

Notes

_____

_____

_____

_____

_____

_____

_____

_____

_____

_____

_____

_____

_____

_____

_____

_____

_____

Chapter Four

Five Steps to Generating Referral After Referral

Generating referrals is important to every business. Today more than ever, obtaining new customers by word-of-mouth marketing is critical to your success. Word-of-mouth marketing happens everywhere, all the time. You may be at a networking event, worshiping at church, or even working out at the gym. We meet people in many different places that could be referral partners or referral sources to help with the growth of our business.

Simply meeting the right person in the right place is not enough, however. There is a process – a proven process – to generating referrals. This process must be followed exactly as it is shown. Skipping any of the steps can result in the referral never happening or at the least make the process more difficult. Follow this process and you will greatly increase the number of referrals you receive and, in turn, increase your income.

1. Identify EXACTLY who is a good referral for you. What industry does this person work in? What is their position? Do you

have the name of a specific person you would like an introduction to? Take the time to perform this step in advance of meeting anybody. Do the thinking; perform the research online; write the information down.

2. When talking to your potential referral partner, make it clear that you will happily do most of the work to make the connection happen. You can provide an email template for them to use so all they have to do is copy, paste, and hit Send. Should they be uncomfortable with making the connection, simply ask their permission to use their name and let you call the referral yourself. All of the other steps to this referral process still apply even if you make the call.

3. Ask the person making the referral what you can do to help them. Who would they like to be connected to? Can you write a testimonial for them on their LinkedIn page? Can you help them market their services through social media? Remember: the Law of Reciprocity always applies. *(Just a note: Most Financial Advisors and Certified Financial Planners can not give or receive testimonials through social media. However, there are other ways of giving and getting testimonials, such as through word of mouth.)*

4. Follow Up. This is the most important part of this process. Call or meet with people you are referred to; and perform with excellence. The reputation of the person who referred you is on the line. Don't let them down. If you have trouble following up, be sure to contact the connector to let them know what happened and what you are doing to rectify the situation. Sometimes they will help make the introduction a "warmer" one.

5. Thank the person that made the referral, especially if it leads to new business or a new referral source. It doesn't have to be anything too fancy. A handwritten note will usually suffice. If the new business generates considerable financial benefits, a steak dinner is certainly a nice way to say thank you to the connector. (Just be sure you're not breaking any industry or ethics rules.)

   This is where most professionals stop. They move on to the next deal, and they forget about how they received this last bit of business. That is a big mistake. And that brings us to the BONUS step in this process.

6. Ask your new client who they know that is just like them, that you could also reach out to. Go to Step 2 above and follow the process. Our best referrals often come from the people we are already doing business with. That's because there's nothing like a raving fan. Treat your current customers well, and they will generate referrals for you.

   As you make getting referrals an important piece of your prospecting process, be sure to reciprocate and give some referrals as well. Give as many or more than you receive.

EXAMPLE EMAIL TEMPLATES TO
PROVIDE TO REFERRAL SOURCES.

Template One:

I want to introduce to you a good friend of mine, _First & Last Name._ She owns and operates _company name_ and she recently mentioned to me that she works with many companies like yours. I immediately thought of you and wanted to make an introduction in case you're interested in having a conversation.

Her company helps _specific solution company provides_. I know your industry has _problem or pain being addressed_ and _First Name_ meets and exceeds all expectations.

She will reach out to you and make the meeting happen.

Template Two:

Joe Novara is a speaker, coach and bestselling author. Many professionals struggle getting enough referrals for their business. Through seminars, workshops and coaching, Joe teaches a proven system for getting more referrals for your business. His clients ultimately meet more prospects, close more sales and make more money.

I know you will enjoy meeting with Joe and learning how he can help you.

Template Three:

I want to introduce you to *First & Last Name*, *Title and Company Name*. *First Name 's* company works with *Industry Type* companies that have document translation needs. I immediately thought of you and wanted to make an introduction in case you're interested in having a conversation. *Company Name* works in been in business for over *# of years* as a *State ie NC*-headquartered company. *First Name* and his staff provide *Service Supplied* that are on time and on budget. To learn more, please see his website at *Website Address*. *First Name* will reach out to you to see if he may be able to help your company.

Template Four:

Hi *First Name,*

I am very happy to introduce you to my friend *First & Last Name* the owner of *Sign Company* in *Town*. She does fantastic work with signage and she can help you with new signage on your office space. For future reference, *First Name* also does amazing work on trade show signage.

Hi *First Name of sign company owner,*

I am happy to introduce you to *First & Last Name*, the owner of *Company Name.* She just moved her office to a new location and she's going to need new signage at her location. I'm going to leave it to the two of you to take it from here. Have a great day and let me know if I can be of any further assistance.

Sincerely,

Joe

Notes

_____

_____

_____

_____

_____

_____

_____

_____

_____

_____

_____

_____

_____

_____

_____

_____

_____

Chapter Five

A Little Gratitude Can Go a Long Way!

I needed a new exhaust manifold for my car. Frank, my mechanic, suggested I take the car to an exhaust specialist, so he referred me to Frick, a company he feels does a good job. When I called Frick to schedule my appointment, I told Janice, the person who answered the phone, that Frank had referred me. She didn't seem to really care. Okay, I figured I'd tell her in person when I arrived. Maybe she was just busy.

I took my car to Frick the next day. After I was checked in, I told Janice again that my mechanic Frank had referred me to them. She simply said, "That's nice."

As I sat down, I was a bit troubled by the fact that she couldn't care less. At around lunch time, the owner of the shop arrived and sat in his office, within earshot. So, I asked Janice again, "Do you folks keep track of the people that refer business to you?"

"No, we get a lot of referrals," she answered.

"That's great," I responded. "Do you at least indicate on the orders which were referrals and which were walk ins?"

35

Again, Janice said no. At that point, Janice began to appear a little annoyed, so I didn't ask again anything else about the referrals.

I would like to point out that the majority of the five hours I was there, Janice spent talking personal issues with the customers or watching TV. She received three to five calls per hour, most of which she complained were telemarketers.

Now I'm not going to tell this man how to run what is obviously a successful business. But during the five hours I was there, at least six people that came in said they had been referred by other mechanics. Clearly they are doing a great job. Instead of chatting or watching TV, however, Janice could just as easily be sending a thank you card or email to the mechanics that are referring business. God knows she has the time!

Hypothetically, let's say a new exhaust specialist opened right down the street from Frick. And the new shop did just as good a job (or even close) as Frick but followed up with a thank you to the mechanics referring business to them. Who do you think will eventually get more business? I'm willing to bet it will be the guy that said thank you.

Always remember to say thank you to those that pass you referrals. It may seem small, but it means a lot. At a minimum, your referral source will feel valued and appreciated.

Notes

_____

_____

_____

_____

_____

_____

_____

_____

_____

_____

_____

_____

_____

_____

_____

_____

_____

_____

Notes

_____

_____

_____

_____

_____

_____

_____

_____

_____

_____

_____

_____

_____

_____

_____

_____

Chapter Six

Don't Be a "Word of Mouth" Tragedy – Help Your Clients to Sing Your Praises

I absolutely hate moving. Ugh!!!! It's one of my top three least favorite things to do. I have moved 7 different times, and I can tell you, not one of those times was any fun. Each time was worse than the last. My last move was the result of a looming divorce. It was stressful. It was emotionally draining. It was physically exhausting. Thank God for good friends.

My friend Tommy moved around the same time, and he had an experience unlike any I have ever had.

It was easy.

I learned about the ease of Tommy's move from his Facebook post. I got Tommy's permission to share his post with you:

"Granted, I don't have much stuff, and I'm only moving one block away, but they packed all my stuff, disassembled my bed frame and a few sets of shelves, moved, unloaded and reassembled my furniture in the new place…all in just over 3 hours. And it is a 3rd floor walk-up at both apartments. Paying by

the hour, my total came in $150 less than the estimate! Pretty sweet! Especially since moving sucks!"

Tommy did not mention the name of the company. Mind you, we are talking about a joyful experience that probably rivals that of a Hot Fudge Sundae. I wanted to know who these masters of happiness were. Who is this mythical company that makes moving an easy, stress-free event?

I don't blame Tommy for not mentioning their name in his post. That's not his job. The point of Tommy's post was to let his friends know that he moved and that it went well. He did that. This moving company clearly has their strengths, but "Word of Mouth Marketing" is not one of them.

What does this have to do with you? Don't be afraid or ashamed to ask your clients to shout your praises from the rooftops. Especially when you have saved them time and money. Provide them with a link to your social media pages and ask them to post a testimonial in at least one. You can then copy and paste their review in other places, including your website.

If you're a solo-preneur, ask you client to write a recommendation on your LinkedIn page. Give them the link to your page so they don't have to search through thirty people with the same name as you. Again, you can then copy and paste the recommendation into your other social media pages and website.

To finish the story with Tommy, we had the following exchange:

Joseph N.: You might want to post the name of the company all over social media. We are quick to do that when a company screws up. It's nicer to do it when they do a great job.

Tommy.: True. See below. I will add a review on yelp.

The company in our story SHOULD have asked Tommy to do that on their own. It's a good thing I was paying attention. Just another day in the life of a Word of Mouth Marketer...

Notes

_____

_____

_____

_____

_____

_____

_____

_____

_____

_____

_____

_____

_____

_____

_____

_____

_____

Chapter Seven

Current Clients –
Forget Them at Your Own Peril

There is nothing more rewarding than receiving a referral from a current client. When someone calls to offer me a speaking engagement based solely on the referral by one of my clients, I feel overwhelmed with appreciation. That means I did a great job for my client, as it is unlikely they would put their reputation on the line by referring someone by whom they were let down. By taking good care of my client, I generated additional business with fairly little effort.

Current clients are not only good sources for new business. They are also good sources of <u>more</u> business. It is far more cost effective when a current client purchases from you or hires you again. It costs on average five times more to obtain a new client than to retain an existing client. Most businesses and salespeople invest countless thousands of dollars into marketing in an effort to win new clients. However, when some of this money is allocated to client appreciation programs, client retention rates increase and in turn, referrals are easier for you to ask for and easier for your clients to make to you.

Show your clients some love by implementing a formal appreciation program. It will also keep you top of mind. There are many ways to keep the appreciation program low-cost. For example, host a small event, with hors d'oeuvres and light refreshments. This brings clients together, and if you're in business-to-business sales, you're in turn providing them an opportunity to meet potential clients and referral sources. You can even do it right in your office to further reduce the cost.

A friend in the promotional products industry personally delivers little bags with freshly baked chocolate chip cookies to the top 20% of his local client base. Low cost. High return!

I heard of a salesman taking his best clients on a fishing excursion for the day to bring them together and to say thank you for their business. He was the top salesperson at his company for years prior to a very happy retirement.

Institute a social media campaign where you post, tag, comment, like and share for your best clients. This is also a great way of showing appreciation. Testimonials cost you little in your time and reward you long term by producing a loyal (and happy) client.

The more time we invest in building solid relationships with our current clients, the more likely they will stay with us and refer business to us. I recently heard from a friend after she lost a big account. Unbeknownst to the two parties, I knew them both personally. For the sake of this story, we'll refer to my friend as Tracy. She complained to me that there had never been a problem with any of the services she provided and that she was also a regular client of the other business. As far as she knew, everything was hunky-dory.

I had been hired to do some short-term coaching by one of the sales reps at the company Tracy lost as a client. While I wasn't trying to gossip, I couldn't help but ask my coaching client why Tracy had lost their business. The sales rep said the owner of the company felt disappointed that he hadn't personally heard from Tracy in almost two years. He felt like she deemed his business unimportant. I reminded my coaching client that Tracy was also a regular customer of the company. "Doesn't that count for something?" I asked. My client explained that the owner works from home and has no idea who comes into the office to purchase their services. All he knew was that Tracy had never made any attempt to contact him. Not even to say hello.

The moral of this story: Stay top-of-mind with clients. If it has been six months or more since you've last seen the person who decides whether you continue getting their business or not, then make sure you reach out to that person. Find out how things are going. What's working? Is there anything you can do to improve what you're doing for them? Find out if there are opportunities for you to refer other business to them. And when you do refer other business to them, make sure the decision maker knows about it. Never take it for granted that the decision maker knows you've been purchasing their products or services or sending them new business.

Lastly, even if it is a business-to-consumer relationship (not B2B), following up is just as important. In some cases, it's even more important. Break out of a transactional mindset and shift to a relationship mindset. It will increase business substantially in the long term. If you're doing a great job, you're creating raving fans and customer loyalty. A relationship mindset will also strengthen future business opportunities.

Follow-up for Success

1. It's your responsibility to follow-up. Not your prospects. What 3 to 5 follow-up methods will you implement into your business immediately?

   01. _____

   02. _____

   03. _____

   04. _____

   05. _____

2. Have an automated system for staying in touch with people. If you're not already utilizing a CRM (Customer Relationship Management System), which one will you begin to use.

3. Address your reasons for not following up and work to eliminate them. That may include hiring a coach or seeking other professional help.
   What is your number one reason for not following up?

   _____

   _____

Continue Next Page

4. Write down who are the top five people/businesses you will
    follow up with until they become a client or tell you a hard
    no. Then engage!

01. _____

02. _____

03. _____

04. _____

05. _____

5. Remember, REJECTION WILL NOT KILL YOU!!!
    It just moves you closer to your next yes!

Follow-up will not only guarantee
you more business.

Follow-up will help you to stand
out above the competition!

Notes

_____

_____

_____

_____

_____

_____

_____

_____

_____

_____

_____

_____

_____

_____

_____

_____

_____

_____

Chapter Eight

Networking Your Way to Business, Friendship and Beyond

Lin Su identified a potential prospect that would make a perfect client for her Chinese interpreting and translation business. The prospect's name is Donna Solomon. After a professional introduction was made by a mutual networking contact via LinkedIn, Lin contacted Donna, setting up a time to meet for coffee. She was very prepared for the meeting, researching Donna's personal likes, schools attended and other organizations she is a member of. After previewing Donna's Facebook page, Lin discovered that they both have two daughters around the same age.

Despite all her preparation, there was one thing that Lin did not prepare for. When Lin and Donna met, they immediately developed a rapport that Lin did not expect. They had so many similarities on a personal level, Lin could see a potential friendship blossoming. She held off bringing up business at that meeting and decided to wait until the next meeting.

They set up another coffee meeting for two weeks later. Lin would again be prepared, and she planned not to get sidetracked.

49

However, the same thing happened again. Lin and Donna talked for two hours without ever mentioning business. As this new friendship was developing, Lin felt unsure about asking for the business anymore. She felt it would be rude to now talk business with someone that had become a friend.

After seeing me speak on Relationship Marketing, Lin called me and we spoke. She shared with me the situation with Donna and how she felt it could damage their new friendship should she ask for business at this point.

Here is what I told Lin, and what I suggest, should you find yourself in the fortunate situation of developing a friendship with a prospect:

01. If you start to develop a friendship with a prospect, Go For It! Developing a personal friendship while networking is one of its greatest benefits. Some of my closest friends have come as a result of business networking. I know a gentleman that moved from Hawaii to North Carolina. Two years later at his wedding, thirty of the fifty people in attendance were friends he made through business networking. He also has a very successful business as a result of those relationships.

02. Do not be embarrassed or afraid to ask for the business, however, you must handle it a little differently due to your friendship. When calling or meeting with your friend/prospect, be very clear right up front that you would like to have a short conversation regarding business. For Lin, it might go something like this. "Donna, do you mind if we take a few minutes to talk about business? Your company could be a perfect client for me, and I would like to talk to you about it."

If Donna agrees (which is likely), Lin should do exactly what she promised: speak about her business and what she can do to help Donna's company — for only a few minutes. If Donna seems receptive to receiving a proposal, Lin should find out how to proceed. Then move back to the things that developed their friendship in the first place.

03. Be prepared for the possibility that your friend/prospect is not receptive to discussing business at this point in the relationship, or does not feel you would be a good vendor for her business. That way, you will not develop resentment and sour the new friendship.

04. Here's the key: If you win the business from your friend/prospect, you MUST provide your absolute best level of respect and service. Remember, there is a personal relationship now on the line here as well. This goes for any business situation where there is some kind of a personal relationship involved.

05. You should set clear boundaries about keeping the personal relationship and the business relationship separate. That will help avoid confusion the next time you meet for coffee to talk about your children and spouses, or if you meet to discuss an upcoming project. That will especially help avoid confusion when it is time to get paid.

In my personal opinion, if you value this relationship and you see that your business is not a good fit with your friend, or you find unresolvable stresses building as a result of the business, offer a solution to help your friend work with one of your competitors. The business will always be temporary, while a good friendship may last a lifetime.

Notes

_____

_____

_____

_____

_____

_____

_____

_____

_____

_____

_____

_____

_____

_____

_____

_____

_____

_____

PART TWO

Prospecting and Sales

JOSEPH NOVARA

Chapter Nine

Looking for Referrals?
Then Answer the Phone and Show Up!

I often wonder why one business does so well, while another almost identical business doesn't make it. There are many factors involved in the failure of a business, many of which are out of the owner's control. However, it is rare that a business succeeds, receiving high quality referrals, without the owner taking intentional steps that lead to its success.

My friend Brian owns a landscaping business in Chapel Hill, North Carolina. In the several years I've known Brian, I've watched his business start from a very small company and grow very quickly into a large, successful organization. I wanted to know what he is doing that makes him so successful amongst several hundred other landscaping companies.

So, I called Brian one day and asked him about the secret to his success. At first, Brian was a little surprised by my question. However, after a little bit of thought, he was able to come up with his answers pretty easily. The first thing he said, which struck a chord with me immediately, was, "We answer our phones. And if we can't answer, we return the call right away."

That is very impressive. Think about that. How often do you call a company, and you are instantly connected to an automated system? Sure, you're promised a call back within 24 hours. Within 24 hours?! Like most folks, I am an "instant gratification" kind of guy, and I want an answer now. Not tomorrow. If you answer my call now, your likelihood of getting my business probably goes up by 90%.

The next thing Brian said, which is equally as important, is that his company shows up, does great work, and stands behind their work. They provide nothing less than high quality work. Brian strives for excellence in his work, and his company's success is proof that they attain that excellence. If you think about it, there is too much competition out there for Brian not to offer his clients the best work and highest level of service.

Brian's work is not the least expensive, yet his phone keeps ringing off the hook. Why? The great customer service his company provides and their high standards of quality produces an endless stream of referrals from enthusiastically happy clients. Not just satisfied clients. Enthusiastically happy clients.

Here are some reasons people pay more for products and services when there are others available at lower prices…

1. The ease of purchasing your product or service.

2. The timely manner in which you perform the service, or your product arrives.

3. There are features to your product that are a "must have".

4. Using your product or services improves the image of the buyer.

5. The long-term ownership of your product or service will save the buyer time or money.

6. Your customer service is easy to reach and more friendly.

7. The price difference isn't worth the hassle.

8. You have a relationship with the customer already.

9. You have other products or services the customer wants or needs.

10. The customer is experiencing rapid growth and values the long-term relationship over short term financial savings.

I suggest we all follow Brian's lead. Always answer your phone. When you can't answer the phone, call back as soon as possible – like today! When you get the order, SHOW UP, do a great job, and stand behind your work. This will lead to enthusiastically happy clients, which will lead to an endless stream of referrals.

(The above list of 10 is based on an article in Inc Magazine titled "10 Reasons Customers Will Pay More" by Geoffrey James)

Notes

_____

_____

_____

_____

_____

_____

_____

_____

_____

_____

_____

_____

_____

_____

_____

_____

_____

_____

_____

Notes

_____

_____

_____

_____

_____

_____

_____

_____

_____

_____

_____

_____

_____

_____

_____

_____

_____

_____

Chapter Ten

Kill the Coffee and Up Your Referrals

Some people reading the title of this chapter will immediately think I am suggesting sacrilegious practices about cutting out coffee. I promise you, I am not talking about cutting out your coffee. I think I could possibly die a miserable death without my coffee. No, I am referring to cutting out "Coffee Meetings". And not all "Coffee Meetings". Just the ones you don't need to be attending.

As somebody who teaches relationship marketing, I sure did get tired of having coffee all the time. It began to feel like everybody I came into contact with wanted to meet with me for coffee. It got to a point where I was having several coffees a day and never getting any business done. Sadly, many of the people I was having coffee with were only having coffee with me because that was the only way they knew how to "appear busy".

After hundreds of coffees and an Inbox full of unanswered emails, it occurred to me that this wasn't working. I needed to change something. Now, when somebody I don't know says, "Let's meet for coffee," my initial reaction is usually, "Let's schedule a phone call first." There are a few exceptions, but for the most part, that is now my response.

As a speaker, coach and author on the subject of relationship marketing, one of the things I encourage my clients to do is to not spin their wheels and waste their time. I need to adhere to that principle myself. I also don't want the people that asked me to coffee to waste their time. You see, it can become a habit to automatically say, "Let's grab coffee." A bad habit, in my not-so-humble opinion.

Why do you want to grab coffee? What do you think we'll accomplish by grabbing coffee? What is going to happen during that coffee meeting that maybe couldn't get accomplished over a 15 minute phone call?

Having a coffee with somebody involves several activities. First, you have to pick a place and a time to have that coffee. If not done immediately upon the first time you met, it could take several emails or texts just to lock in a time that works for both parties. You also have to drive to and from the place where the meeting will be held. Now you're committed to anywhere from 60 to 90 minutes of your day. GONE. And often during that coffee, you realize, "This is a complete waste of my time. This person will never be able to refer me business, nor will I ever be able to refer her business. Why am I here?"

You could have figured that out over a short phone call. If during a 15 minute phone call I realize this is somebody I want to get to know better, THEN I might say, "Hey! Let's grab coffee! I see we have a lot more to talk about."

Take control of your time. Don't allow others to dictate your schedule. Having coffee several times a day means that you are either letting somebody dictate your schedule or even worse, you are avoiding the real work that will help grow your business.

Unless, of course, your business is selling coffee! Then have lots and lots of coffee meetings.

As you may have experienced, some people are persistent about meeting in person. Fine. But if they truly want to meet, they will have to work around my schedule and meet at a location that is convenient to me. Sometimes I will stack two or three coffee meetings around a specific meeting I already have scheduled with a client or referral partner. Prior to the meetings, I will communicate clearly with each person how long our meeting will last. That is so there will be no surprises when I have to stop or the other person I may be expecting walks in.

Reserve your time for your referral partners, referral sources, prospects, clients and vendors. If you have a system for strategically giving and receiving referrals, then you won't have to spin your wheels, wasting money and a lot of time in frivolous coffee meetings. Instead, by meeting with the right people, your time will be well spent, and you will earn more money.

Notes

Chapter Eleven

The Investment of Closing a Sale

How much are you willing to invest in closing a sale? One minute of your time? Ten minutes of your time? How about ten hours of your time? The amount of time you invest will often be commensurate with the size of the sale.

Retail sales involve a very short sales cycle. In some cases, you can blink and it's over. As you probably know, most retail salespeople are paid an hourly wage. At the end of the week, they get a paycheck that they can spend immediately. No questions asked.

Commission sales is an entirely different story. For example, real estate transactions involve a much longer sales cycle. From the time a home is listed to the time the realtor sees the money in the bank can often be months. Most real estate salespeople work on straight commission – if the property doesn't sell, they don't get paid. However, if the property does sell, the pay is often significant for the amount of time invested. As a general rule, the higher the risk and time commitment involved, the higher the pay.

You, as a person in sales, must decide what your time is worth. How much of your time are you willing to invest in getting the sale? Also, how much of your time are you willing to risk on a deal that may fall apart?

When I was starting out in sales, I was guilty of getting caught up with prospects that did not have a real need at the time of engagement. In some of those cases, these prospects had no real intention of purchasing at all. I'm embarrassed to say it happened many times during my early years. It was a function of experience and qualifying my prospect. As I gained more experience, my skills at qualifying a prospect improved greatly.

A key component to qualifying a lead is simple: ask questions. A few questions you may want to ask when qualifying a prospect are:

1. Do you have a need now?

2. If not now, when?

3. What is your budget?

4. Are the funds available or will you need a lender?

5. Are you the primary decision maker, or is there another person or group who must make the final decision?

6. What is the pain, problem or challenge you want to overcome as a result of our work together?

While there are many other questions you will want to ask that are buyer and industry specific, if the prospect can't or won't answer these five basic qualifying questions, you may want to move on to one that will.

By asking qualifying questions, you will improve your time management and, consequently, you will improve your income. This requires discipline on your part. It also requires confidence in your belief that the services you offer are of real value that you can stand behind. Sales can be a lot of fun and very rewarding. Put in some work by doing a little research and asking the right questions. In turn, you will save your prospect and yourself time and move closer to what you both want: a sale.

What are some additional qualifying questions you can ask your prospect when identifying their needs? Keep them handy until you have them memorized.

Notes

Chapter Twelve

What is the Volume of Your "Sphere of Influence"?

I remember once driving to the store with my daughter Sophia when she was 14 years old. She challenged me. "Dad, do you know the formula to determine the volume of a sphere?"

The last time I was asked that question had been more than thirty years earlier, so I sadly had to admit I hadn't a clue. (In my defense, I probably didn't know the answer thirty years before then either.)

She confidently responded, "Four thirds, times pi, times r cubed!" ($^4/_3 \times \pi \times r^3 = V$). I was proud and impressed by my girl.

Later that day, inspired by Sophia's question, I wondered if there was a formula for the volume of a "sphere of influence"? I called my friend and mentor Earl Hadden to discuss this thought. He immediately hit me with the word "exposure." The more exposure you have in the marketplace, the bigger your sphere of influence. The more content you provide through more channels, the more exposure you will have.

As Earl and I discussed it further, it became clear that another important element of the formula is your referral network. Sales great and Guinness World Record holder Joe Girard claims that, on average, every person knows 250 people they can influence with their opinions and experiences. So, in essence, when you make a new business connection, you have increased your network by an additional 250 people.

Earl and I hashed it out for a couple of hours and in the end, we came up with what we felt was a pretty good method to figuring out our own spheres of influence.

Here is the formula for the "Volume of Sphere of Influence":

$$(N \times 250) + (C \times P) = V$$

Where N = Number of people in your <u>Referral Network</u> (referral sources, referral partners, clients, friends, family members, fans, organization members, employees, your attorneys, your CPA, etc.)
C = Number of <u>Channels of Communication</u> (website, blog, seminars/workshops, social media outlets, ie. Linkedin, Twitter, Facebook, Pinterest, etc.)
P = Number of times your <u>Communication Pieces</u> are read, watched or heard, (views, click throughs, downloads, retweets, likes, printouts, LinkedIn views)
V = <u>Volume</u> of the Sphere of Influence.

It's all quantifiable. Each person you bring into your referral network means that through secondary connections, you add 250 people on average to your network. Add two more people, you've grown your network by an additional 500 people. Add 10 new people, you've just grown your network by an additional 2500 people.

The more content you write, the more videos you produce, the more audios you record, and the more live seminars you perform all increase your communication methods to get your message out to the public. Then you strategically push these communication pieces out to the market and increase your exposure.

For example, if I stop producing written content, stop producing videos, stop attending business events, and stop doing workshops or seminars, my sphere of influence will shrink, eventually disappearing into obscurity. However, each time a person reads one of my LinkedIn posts, or purchases a copy of my book "Intentional Networking", or watches one of my videos, my sphere of influence grows larger.

Eventually the "compound effect" comes into play. As demonstrated in Darren Hardy's book of the same name, *"The Compound Effect" is a reminder of the law of cause and effect and how you can make yourself accountable for your choices. The Compound Effect is the ripple effect you get from the choices you make.*

When that happens, you will experience explosive growth, and all your efforts begin to pay off in the form of new clients, greater exposure in the marketplace, and increased profits.

Don't ever become complacent about strengthening and growing your network.

Some tips for keeping your sphere of influence healthy:

- Make it easy for those in your network to refer you. You do that by having an easy to remember elevator speech that they can easily share with people in their network.

- Don't stop creating new content. When writing blog posts and articles, short and sweet is your friend, in my opinion. Even writing 300 to 500 words should not be terribly difficult. While SEO experts suggest that articles be written at between 1500 and 2000 words for online searchability, I still prefer the shorter articles because based on my own research, consumers are more likely to read shorter articles. I have also found the average business owner/salesperson is more willing to write an article of 500 words or less because they don't find it quite as intimidating.

  All that being said, if you are writing posts and articles specifically with the intention of driving traffic to your website and don't really care if it gets read completely, then you'll want to get the word count over 1500. If you're not a very good writer or you just don't have the time, you have options. The easiest option is to hire a content writer to write for you. Tell this person what you want them to write about and let them do all the work. Another option is to record yourself speaking on a specific topic you would have written about. Then hire someone to transcribe your recording. After a little bit of editing on your part, you'll have an article ready to go.

- Use your phone to create one-minute videos you can upload to Instagram, Facebook and your YouTube channel. Or live stream videos of yourself or others using Facebook Live or similar technologies. Creating content has never been easier.

- Be sure to have professional looking social media accounts, whether it's LinkedIn, Facebook, Twitter, Instagram or Pinterest.

- Lastly, ensure your website (or blog) is fresh and mobile friendly.

The next time my daughter feels the need to ask me a question, I hope it's something easier like, "Should we have pizza or Chinese for dinner tonight?"

Notes

_____

_____

_____

_____

_____

_____

_____

_____

_____

_____

_____

_____

_____

_____

_____

_____

_____

_____

_____

Chapter Thirteen

No Soliciting -
Hello, Is Anybody Home?

From the beginning of time, many people involved in sales had to knock on doors or do drop-ins. When done correctly, door-to-door sales can be one of the most rewarding forms of sales.

Imagine thousands of years ago, a caveman who had fire to sell had a product that all the other cavemen and cavewomen needed and wanted. This salesperson would stop by a neighborhood cave with torch in hand after recent rainstorms had flooded the cave and drowned out the family fire. When the cave had become cold and damp, and meat couldn't get cooked, it was unlikely he'd have doors slammed in his face. Or worse yet, any boulders dropped on his head. It was an easy sale. There was a need. He identified the need. He filled the need. He was probably paid in food and some form of clothing. Maybe even protection.

In the Bible we read of tent salesmen. We read of idol salespeople. Joseph and Jesus may have even been traveling carpenters, going from town to town, selling their services one home, one business and one palace at a time.

Over time, almost anything a person could purchase in a store could probably be sold door to door. Some of these products and services have been medicine, books, encyclopedia sets, vacuum cleaners, financial services, beds, art, printing, cookies, candy, religion and on and on.

Through the years, many salespeople learned deceptive tactics for selling these products or services, lying to trusting people that the magic potion they were selling would heal all ailments. Many of these salespeople became known as snake oil salesmen.

They're taught scripts and other pushy methods that make unsuspecting homeowners and business owners feel defenseless when caught off guard. Consumers often purchase something they don't really need or want simply to avoid saying no or just to get rid of the salesperson. Deceptive and rude tactics like these are what began making people wary of door-to-door salespeople.

Of course, not all people selling door to door are rude or deceptive. It's my belief that most are doing so with a great sense of integrity and care. However, all it takes is for one person to get scammed. Then everyone in the neighborhood and surrounding areas is going to know about it: *"Beware the man or woman selling door to door."*

So with all the negative repercussions of door-to-door sales, what are the positives? It can be more difficult for someone to behave rudely when a live human being is standing right there in front of them. They may not purchase your product or service, but because you can see their face and they can see yours, it's more likely they will politely say no. *(This is not always the case, but if you do it often enough, you'll develop a thicker skin. See the story titled "Finding Karen" in my book "Intentional Networking.)*

As salespeople, it's our responsibility to remember that we've shown up unannounced. We've just interrupted this person's day. If they were performing an important task, we may have broken their concentration. If someone does act rude or curt when I have stopped in cold, I remind myself of this. The ruder the person is, the more likely it is that this person is just having a bad day and you happened to show up at exactly the wrong time.

The more doors we knock on, the more we increase the averages that we will encounter someone who is rude. And remember, this is the exception to the norm, but it will happen. The more doors you knock on, the more often it will happen. If knocking on doors is where you see your greatest success, then I honestly hope you encounter many rude people because that only means you've also knocked on the doors of many kinder people.

I'm not going to pretend I don't hate rejection. Fear of rejection may be the number one thing preventing salespeople from being successful, and when I first started in sales many years ago, I didn't realize rejection would be so much a part of the job. I came to learn later it's actually a huge part of the job. And on some days, it feels like the only part.

When I started selling real estate, I stared into the eyes of rejection every day. I worked in downtown Brooklyn, NY, where most property sales are condos and co-ops. I went home some nights feeling extremely beaten down and depressed from having been told NO so many times.

Then one day I thought about my years on the dating scene. I was a shy introvert, yet finding a date was rarely an issue for me. I always had a girlfriend, and usually she was pretty. Considering that I was short, average looking, and shy, how did I do that? I'll tell you how. The law of averages. If I talked to enough girls, sooner or later one of them would like me. And then sooner or later, I would like one in return. It was a numbers game.

I realized that sales in business was very similar to the dating scene. It was all a numbers game. If I talked to enough people who needed my services, and I was honest and came from a place of integrity and authenticity, I would close more sales. The fewer people I talked to, the fewer sales I made. Conversely, the more people I talked to, the more sales I made. That meant the more NOs I received, the more YESs I received as well.

My friend Craig is a master telecommunications salesman and loves hearing the word NO. He says that for every NO he receives, he figures he earns $50.00. He makes 100 door knocks per week. Yes, that number is correct — 100. Door knocks. So, he hears NO a lot. But he is enthusiastic about what he does. And very good at it, too. There are dozens of salespeople in the same local market as Craig, yet few are anywhere near as successful.

You may be wondering how to meet the same success, especially when businesses you'd like to approach have the dreaded "NO SOLICITING" sign at the entrance. When I was selling printing, I learned a very simple method for approaching these businesses. Most salespeople stop short when they see that sign, and that's what the business owner is hoping for. But many of these businesses have their own salespeople out on the road doing the same thing, so someone stopping in—while at times annoying— is not completely shocking.

My mindset was this, when I showed up and saw that sign, there was no way I wasn't going in there. And, I was going to do it in a way that was quick and painless for the gatekeeper or business owner. I'd say, "Hi, I don't mean to bother you. Who is the person I should call regarding the printing for your company?" If they said it was Mr. Smith, I'd ask if Mr. Smith had a business card I could take. If not, I made sure to write down Mr. Smith's name as soon as I left.

I'd do additional research later and follow up with a call to Mr. Smith. However, if the person I first met identified themselves as the person who ordered the printing, I'd want to give them an out. "Well, I just stopped in unexpected, so I don't want to bother you. When is a better time for me to give you a call to chat?" This method worked well for me many times.

So, while I still don't like rejection, I recognize that it's necessary. And I have to admit that, as much as I hate hearing NO, I really like hearing YES a whole lot more. It makes hearing NO so worth it. If you are in sales and can improve your income by knocking on some doors, then go out there and get that next NO!

Notes

_____

_____

_____

_____

_____

_____

_____

_____

_____

_____

_____

_____

_____

_____

_____

_____

_____

Chapter Fourteen

Death By Social Media

I was so grateful when the election of 2016 was over, and the inauguration was complete. Over that previous several months, as both sides of the political spectrum threw knives at each other on social media, I kept my opinions to myself. That was – until one afternoon – when I finally chimed in – and completely embarrassed myself.

My childhood friend Brian had posted something on Facebook regarding one group of people that I didn't feel was accurate. A group of people that I actually do NOT side with. However, I felt compelled to comment. I used foul language and came across very angry. In doing so, I contradicted everything I try to teach my audiences and coaching clients about collaborating and being positive and supportive of others.

Brian responded to my comment. He was not angry, but more like disappointed. And surprised – surprised that this response had come from me. I answered his comment, pretending I didn't understand why he was surprised. But I knew that I did understand his disappointment and confusion.

For the next ten minutes, as I reflected on my exchange with Brian, I felt very uneasy. Then I realized just how wrong I was. As soon as I admitted to myself that I was wrong, I went back to Brian's Facebook page and deleted my negative comment.

But I didn't stop there. I sent Brian a private message and apologized to him for my comments on his page. I told him that I was aware that the manner in which I presented my comments were wrong. We have known each other for over 40 years, and we have been through a lot of good times and bad times together. Needless to say, all was forgiven very quickly. In fact, we ended up having a good friendly conversation through chat for the next 30 minutes. Before signing off, we reminded each other that we are very important to each other.

That is the key. That is why I use social media. That is who I want to be. I am human, and I make mistakes daily. I'd be a liar if I said that at times I don't get frustrated by others' political views. But I have been blessed with the ability to recognize my mistakes and to make amends quickly. And that's what I did with Brian that day.

From a business standpoint, what if one of my clients or prospects had seen my comment? From that time forward, he or she would question everything I say and teach about motivation and helping others. Everything I have ever said about integrity and reciprocity would be discarded as just hype to sell books and coaching programs. It would have been DEATH BY SOCIAL MEDIA! Death for my reputation and death for my business. No, that is not who I am or what I want.

From that day forward, I committed to only ever using social media to build people up. To encourage others. To inform without being hurtful to others. And to share as much humor as possible. I have learned that nothing beats a good belly laugh.

I was once told that if it isn't helpful, if it doesn't inspire or it isn't kind, then don't say it. That day shortly after the election, I needed that reminder. Thank you, Brian, for calling me out on my mistake. That's what real friends do for each other.

Notes

Chapter Fifteen

Be a Video Superstar

When it comes to increasing awareness of you, your company, and your brand online, video content dominates. It took me a while to buy in to the importance of video content for a business. Many of the reasons relate to vanity. I don't like the way I look on video; I don't like my voice on video; my shirt collars never look quite right; the scenery behind me never looks professional enough. I can go on and on about all the things I don't like about doing video.

What I do like about video is that my target audience likes my videos. Many of my peers like my videos. Even some of the friends I grew up with on Long Island leave positive comments and compliment my videos. Of course, there is still the occasional knucklehead who comments like we're still in high school. (You know who you are!)

Without a doubt, videos have increased my brand awareness. They have also allowed me to communicate my message to thousands of people I may not have reached through written blogs or creating clever posts on social media.

Many people wrongly assume that it is expensive and/or complicated to create good videos. Not so. If you have a smart phone, you're half way there. Fortunately, my phone has a high-quality camera, so the actual creation of a video is easy and looks pretty good. It took me two hours recording my first video to get an acceptable two minute segment of me talking about relationship marketing.

I was trying to make it perfect. I was trying to sound and look natural and polished. I was so frustrated by the end of the two hours, I was ready to throw my phone on the floor and jump up and down on it. Luckily for my phone, though, the final product was decent. Not good, but decent for sure. And that was confirmed when I posted it on social media and emailed it to my network – I received very good feedback.

As I contemplated making more videos, I thought about the videos I was watching on social media and on YouTube. Aside from twelve minute Gary Vaynerchuck videos, whenever a video is longer than two and a half minutes, I rarely watch the whole thing. Heck, I even want the DIY car repair videos to be five minutes or less!

My first few videos on relationship marketing or sales tips ran between two and five minutes in length. They improved the more comfortable I got doing them. Soon I realized, though, that I would be better off recording shorter, one minute videos. Again, I found myself wanting to watch shorter, more succinct videos. Therefore, my audience probably wanted the same thing. So that became my focus.

In creating one minute videos, I learned something else: The shorter the video, the more difficult it is to get my point across with clarity. I only have sixty seconds. How much can someone say in sixty seconds? (Unless you're a trained auctioneer.) After a lot of practice and frustration, though, I learned I can actually say quite a bit. And I can convey my message clearly. Did I mention it took a lot of practice and frustration? Well, it did! And it has paid off in spades.

You might be wondering, "How does he choose what to talk about with only one minute?" I start my videos by identifying a problem (in the sales or marketing arena). Then I spend 10 to 20 seconds discussing a solution. I follow that up with 10 to 20 seconds discussing 1 or 2 benefits of that solution. Lastly, I take a few seconds at the end of the video to recap the problem, solution, and benefits. I've enjoyed this format, but you should use what's comfortable for you and, more importantly, what your target audience enjoys and finds helpful. My one minute videos have been very well received, and they have helped me grow my reach consistently.

You may also be wondering about where I put my video. First, I upload my video to YouTube. That is where my video will reside (or in technical terms, where it will be "hosted"). In the process of doing so, I create and add a title, a description, and a handful of hashtags. These give the viewer a sense of what to expect from the video. They also help my audience find my content more easily.

Next, I copy the YouTube link and share it (along with a blurb) in almost every LinkedIn sales and marketing group I am in. I want to reach a large audience, and I find that LinkedIn groups are where I get the most traction. I belong to and participate in

30 or more LinkedIn groups. (Read more about the effective use of LinkedIn in the chapter on social media.)

I also share the YouTube link of my video in a post on my home page. I usually add two to five hashtags to the post. That will help drive decision makers and influencers to the video when they search online for the terms in the hashtags.

Next, I upload the video to Instagram, where I use 10 to 20 hashtags with the post. Pro Tip: use the "send to TWITTER" feature in Instagram to also share the post through Twitter, but while saving yourself a little bit of time. I have watched my Instagram network grow very quickly since beginning this strategy.

Finally, I use Facebook like a hybrid of my Linkedin and Instagram strategies. I upload my video to my business page in Facebook and add three to five hashtags for people searching for content related to my topic. I was taught that uploading my video directly to Facebook (not the YoutTube link) increases my organic reach, meaning Facebook rewards me by allowing more people to see my video that I worked so darn hard on. Then, to help with my local brand awareness, I share the YouTube link to my video in a handful of Facebook groups I belong to.

As far as how many videos to make or how often I post, as of this writing, I record and post two to three videos per week. On days I don't post a video I post other types of content. (Read more about that in the chapter on social media.) As with any type of online content, however, consistency is the key. Decide what your publication schedule is going to be and follow it. Whether it is one video a day or one video a month, stick to your schedule.

Not only will that help you practice your video making and sharing skills, but it will help you build up a library of content, which in turn will help you reach a larger audience. Moreover,

you may find that customers or colleagues grow to expect or rely on seeing new video content from you.

Using video as part of my marketing and business development strategy has many benefits. But don't just take my word for it. Here are some interesting and insightful stats on video content that I pulled from a 2019 Forbes article:

1. By 2019, global consumer Internet video traffic will account for *80% of all consumer Internet traffic* (Source: SmallBizTrends)

2. Facebook generates **8 billion video views** on average per day (Source: Social Media Today)

3. According to YouTube, mobile video consumption rises 100% every year (Source: Hubspot)

4. 55% of people watch videos online every day (Source: Digital Information World)

5. 92% of mobile video consumers share videos with others (Source: RendrFx)

6. **90% of users** say that product videos are helpful in the decision making process (Source: Hubspot)

7. Social video generates *1200% more shares* than text and images combined (Source: SmallBizTrends)

8. Video posts on Facebook have **135% greater organic reach** than photo posts (Source: Social Media Today)

9. A video on a landing page can *increase conversation rates by 80%* (Source: Unbounce)

10. After watching a video, **64% of users are more likely to buy** a product online (Source: Hubspot)

11. Companies using video enjoy 41% more web traffic from search than companies not using video (Source: SmallBizTrends)

12. 59% of senior executives agree that if both text and video are available on the same topic on the same page, they prefer to watch the video (Source: Digital Information World)

13. People *spend 3 times longer* watching a live social video compared to a video that has been prerecorded (Source: Social Media Today)

14. Video in an email leads to **200-300% increase** in click-through rates (Source: Hubspot)

15. Top 3 most effective types of video content: Customer testimonials (51%); Tutorial videos (50%); Demonstration videos (49%) (Source: Curata)

16. A whopping **80% of users recall a video ad** they viewed in the past 30 days (Source: Hubspot)

17. 67% of marketers found video marketing "somewhat successful" (Source: Digital Information World)

I would also like to highlight that video is more personal/human, video forms relationships and video makes your product more relatable.

Your business will reap many benefits from developing and implementing a plan for video creation, posting, sharing, and marketing. Whether you decide to create DIY videos, testimonial videos or informational videos, you will see the importance of videos in your marketing strategy through consistency. It is a process – which takes time.

Don't expect one video to make a difference (although if done well enough, it could go viral). Don't expect four or five videos to do the trick. Focus on being consistent. When you're consistently creating and sharing new videos, and your message is equally as consistent, you will develop and grow your network. Patience is the key. It always is.

Notes

_____

_____

_____

_____

_____

_____

_____

_____

_____

_____

_____

_____

_____

_____

_____

_____

_____

_____

Chapter Sixteen

The Return of the Pony Express

When I began working in the printing industry back in 1986, direct mail marketing was one of the most aggressive forms of marketing to a specific demographic. Much has changed in the past 30 plus years. The pervasiveness of the home computer led to the internet and communicating through email, which then led to marketing on the internet and via email. This led many businesses to move much of their marketing dollars away from printed material and to online marketing.

During almost 30 years in the printing industry, including as an owner of my own company for 5 of those years, I heard many times that print was dead. I heard it so often, at times I started to believe it myself. I have been out of the industry for a few years now, and I can assure you that print is far from dead.

I can also assure you that direct mail marketing is alive and well and getting great results for businesses. Because of an endless tidal wave of unsolicited email marketing and social media marketing, the general public has become desensitized to much of that marketing. Yes, it may be in their line of sight when they check their Facebook page or Instagram feed, but most people have trained their brain to simply ignore those ads. (I have.)

That would explain the resurgence of direct mail marketing in the past few years.

While my generation, Generation X, learned to flip through their stack of mail and immediately throw away most direct mail, studies show that 25% of Millennials find reading direct mail enjoyable. They like having something physical to touch, feel, and hold. Depending on the direct mail piece, it may even have a "pleasant scent" to it. These sensory experiences generate positive emotions and a strong motivation to purchase the products and services offered.

Therefore, in today's world, it is very important for a company to create a marketing strategy that utilizes both targeted digital ads and direct mail marketing pieces.

A direct mail piece can feel very personal, as if it was written only for me. Especially when it addresses a problem I am experiencing or fills a need I have. While I will admit to throwing away most direct mail, I still love a good offer. Especially if it's for a restaurant I already patronize.

The more personalized the piece, the more likely your prospect is to act on it. Include attractive pictures that force people to pay attention. If room allows, include a testimonial – it boosts credibility. However, please don't try to fit your entire product line onto one postcard or brochure. Keep the message focused. The more complicated the piece, the more likely it will go right from the mailbox to the recycling bin.

Don't forget the call to action. What do you want me to do when

I receive your direct mail piece? Don't make me figure out what it is you are hoping I will do. The call to action should be clear and concise. Here are some examples of calls to action you might use:

Call now to receive your free sample.

Try it for 30 days, risk free!

Come in and enjoy a free appetizer on us!

The more unique the design of your piece, the more attention it will get. For example, you can use special die cuts. I once responded to a piece sent to me by a local car dealership that was shaped like a car. All I had to do was call in, tell them my special number on the piece, and find out what I won. There was a chance of winning a new car. Instead, I won a FitBit, and I was still pretty darn happy.

When I went to pick up my FitBit, the dealership was packed with what I assumed were other winners. The sales rep asked me if I wanted to look at any cars. I wasn't in the market for a car at the time and didn't want to take the salesman away from a real prospect. However, I could see that there were many people going for test rides that day. I'm willing to bet they sold many cars as a result of that ad campaign.

To this day, when I drive past that dealership, I only have positive thoughts about it. So clearly, they had an emotional impact on me that could one day result in a sale for them. And it was all because they invested in a car-shaped postcard that they sent to me in the U.S. Mail.

Notes

PART THREE
More Intentional Networking

JOSEPH NOVARA

Chapter Seventeen

The Networking Introvert

I was so quiet and shy as a kid, one of the girls that hung out in my group of friends used to tease me, calling me retarded. Sometimes I found it painful to speak to the friends of my friends, let alone to people I didn't know. Once I got to know you, I was okay, but that could take a long time.

I followed my father into the printing industry at the age of eighteen. Who would have thought a shy guy like me would eventually go into sales. I know my father would have never believed it. My mother always struggled believing it until the day she died. Yet here I am, over 25 years later still doing sales.

To be quite honest with you, I did not realize I was doing sales when I first started though. All I was doing was stopping at other local printing companies to tell them I had a computer at home and I could do some typesetting and design for them. Not many people had home computers at that time, so it made me a little bit special. It was an easy sale.

As time went on, I began to get some of my own printing clients. Most of my clients were my friends and family, but I was getting paid. Again, an easy sale.

After I moved to Brooklyn, New York I decided I wanted to make a career change from printing. I chose the real estate industry. While getting my real estate license was very easy, making money at real estate was not quite as easy. I learned very quickly that as a shy introvert, I was going to need a strategy if I was going to be successful.

The first thing I did after about a month working at a real estate office was I picked up the phone one day and began to call all of my friends and family members within a 20-mile vicinity of where I lived. I explained to them my career change and told them that if they were considering putting their home on the market or knew somebody that was putting their home on the market, I would greatly appreciate an introduction. I also suggested that they let me know if they were looking to move themselves.

My sister-in-law immediately listed an apartment with me to rent in Brooklyn. Several of my local friends also came to me that happened to be looking to upgrade where they were living. Every single person I sold or rented an apartment to in Brooklyn, I would ask them to please refer me to at least one person that they know.

Nobody told me that what I was doing was called *networking*. I had no idea that's what I was doing. But guess what? I was networking and it was the back door to selling that led to this shy kid's success. I didn't have to be pushy or aggressive or do any cold callings. I was selling by relationship.

Real estate in New York City is not always a very nice business and I eventually went back into the printing industry after my first daughter was born. I wanted more sanity and to spend more time with her.

But wouldn't you know it, the desire to sell began to call to me again. While working at this company as one of the managers, I also became a salesperson for the company, reaching out to my network of friends, family and church members for printing opportunities.

There were times when all eight presses at the company I was working for had my orders running on them, all at the same time. You can say my method of relationship selling was working out well.

After moving to North Carolina, I bought an existing printing company. Unfortunately, it was two months before the great recession of 2008. Within six months, we lost close to 50% of our client base.

That's when I truly learned the power of networking and referral partnerships. And it changed my life and business forever.

I was invited to attend and joined a BNI chapter. I immediately began to see my sales increase. Over the next four years, through networking, I was able to bring our sales back to the numbers they had been before we purchased the company.

I began to feel a calling to help people learn how to grow their businesses through networking.

I decided I would become a speaker to share my knowledge on growing a business by referral through relationship marketing. I immediately called the local chamber of commerce and told them I wanted to put on a lunch and learn to teach people about networking. Surprisingly, they were very receptive. That day, I began writing my first speech.

On July 3rd, 2013 I gave my first professional presentation. As a result, I was offered other opportunities to speak for other groups and organizations.

My speaking mentor, Sharon Anita Hill told me I had to write a book. So, I did. In November of 2014, Intentional Networking was published and went on to become an Amazon Best Seller.

I also hired a marketing coach early on. He suggested I wrap all my learning into a coaching program.

I thought, "Me? A coach?"

The thought of coaching others scared me. But over several months, he and I developed a structured coaching program around the best of what I had learned and discovered over the past 25 years. We titled the coaching program, "The Referral Marketing Success System", eventually offering it in one on one and group formats.

The next thing I needed to do was develop confidence to share it with others. Once I started getting clients and realized I was good at coaching and started getting very positive testimonials, I haven't looked back.

I love helping people. I love to have people from the audiences of my speaking engagements and my coaching clients tell me that after trying something different that they learned from me, they've seen a steady increase in the number of high quality referrals they're receiving. That's why I do what I do. I strongly believe in the laws of reciprocity. I cannot express to you how much I have gained as a result of what I have given. Honestly, it's remarkable.

Notes

_____

_____

_____

_____

_____

_____

_____

_____

_____

_____

_____

_____

_____

_____

_____

_____

_____

Chapter Eighteen

Clear Skies and 100% Visibility - A Sales Pro's Dream

If a tree falls in the forest and no LIVING thing is around to hear it, did it really make a sound? Honestly, I have no idea. What I do know is this. If you build an awesome business and nobody knows it exists, you will probably close your doors much sooner than later.

In sales, visibility is very important to stay on your target markets radar. Networking is a great way to do that. And don't only network at your local chamber of commerce (while I do recommend that highly). Network where your target market is networking. Join an organization or association related to your target market.

For instance, a mortgage broker can benefit greatly from joining the local Realtors Association. A sales pro in life insurance may benefit from joining the local restaurant owner's association. The next step after joining is to get involved, volunteer and be of service. Dr Ivan Misner built his multi-national organization BNI on the principal of reciprocity.

Know who your target market is, where they are congregating and be very visible to them. 100% Visibility.

Notes

_____

_____

_____

_____

_____

_____

_____

_____

_____

_____

_____

_____

_____

_____

_____

_____

_____

_____

Notes

_____

_____

_____

_____

_____

_____

_____

_____

_____

_____

_____

_____

_____

_____

_____

_____

_____

Chapter Nineteen

FORM Relationships and Grow Your Network

It surprises me how often people tell me they don't know what to say during conversations at networking events. Lord knows I still struggle with it myself, despite years of training and well over a thousand events. I had been invited to attend a very large event to celebrate the launch of a new convention center in Chapel Hill, NC. When I walked in, there were hundreds of people I DID NOT KNOW! I wanted to leave, and I wanted to leave fast. But I know that meeting new people is the best way for me to grow my business. So that's just what I did – I stayed and met many new people.

In my book "Intentional Networking" there is a chapter titled "Join in on the Conversation" that gives a demonstration on six words that help you during conversations. Here is an excerpt from the chapter..........

"So remember, when attending an event that has a networking element to it, focus more on listening. I like to follow the Who, What, Where, When, Why and How model (WWWWWH). When you are trying to learn about a new prospect, you can keep him talking all night if you keep asking questions that

start with one of the WWWWWH's. Start off with these six questions: "Who do you work for?" "What do you do there?" "Where is the business located?" "When did you start at this company?" "Why do you do work in this profession?" "How long have you been doing it?" Now you have the first six questions to start a conversation with almost anyone you meet when networking. If you find yourself stuck during a conversation, try to think of a question that could start with one of the WWWWWH's."

But wait, there's more!

My great friend and mentor for my speaking business, Sharon Hill, who taught me the 5WH technique also taught me an addendum to the technique. It's called FORM, an acronym for Family, Organization, Recreation and Motivation.

When asking Who, What, Where, When, Why, and How questions, keep to FORM and keep it simple. You don't have to follow the order of the acronym. Just develop questions based on one of those words as they come up in the conversation. Some of my examples may seem simple or even silly out of context, but many of these questions come up naturally during networking conversations — as long as you focus more on listening than on being heard.

Family: How many children do you have *(only if they bring this up first)?* Where are you from? Where do you live? What does your spouse do? To avoid sounding creepy, try not to ask where the children go to school.

Organization: Where do you work? What got you into that line of business? Why did you join that particular rotary club? Do you belong to any associations? If you're trying to win over a new prospect, you may want to avoid asking where they go to church or synagogue. Unless, of course, they mention it first.

<u>Recreation</u>: What sports do you like? When did you start jogging? How often do you exercise? Where do you like to go on vacation? Why do you prefer the mountains? What are your favorite kinds of books to read?

<u>Motivation</u>: What motivates you? Who gives you the most motivation in your life? How do you turn around a bad day? Why are you trying to reach that goal?

I love having a simple system that helps me continue speaking to people when I'm feeling overwhelmed, shy or just plain cranky. And the best part: the system works!

So, the next time you're at an event and you're not feeling at the top of your game, but you still have to network and speak to people you don't know, just try FORM with a side of 5WH.

Notes

Chapter Twenty

Networking... Is it Easy?
With Some Hard Work It Is

Is networking easy? You bet it is! Does networking require hard work? You bet it does! (After all, the word "networking" includes the word "work".)

Sure, networking can be very easy. You show up at a business event. Put on your name tag. Maybe use your drink ticket to get your free adult beverage, hoping someone will give you theirs so you can have a second drink. Then maybe there's some free food, most often donated by a sponsor of the event, whom you never meet. You then walk around collecting business cards. Having conversations that don't go anywhere, without any purpose. And then you go home, throw the stack of business cards in a drawer, and forget about the people you met. Yes, that was easy.

If that is how you are networking, you are wasting your time and the time of the others at the event.

Let's take the same scenario, but also add a little bit of work to it. You don't just go to any event. You do a little research to find an event that will have others in attendance that resemble your current best client. Before the event, you set a goal for how many new contacts you will make at the event. You even go so far as to look online at who some of the attendees will be, and you do a little research on them ahead of time. You connect on Linkedin with two of those on the list, telling them you look forward to meeting them at the event. You think of a few specific questions for each of them, so it will be easier to begin the conversation with them.

When you arrive at the event, you put on your name tag and begin to observe the room. You may feel a little uncomfortable at first because there are so many people there, so you warm up by speaking to a couple of the sponsors at their tables. Sponsors appreciate when people come over to talk to them. That's why they invested in their sponsorship in the first place — to make new connections. Be sure to ask the sponsor questions about their product or service. Don't go into sales mode trying to convince them to purchase from you. They paid for their spot at this event. If the sponsor brings the conversation to learning about your business, that's great and I say jump in. However, if the sponsor doesn't about you, show continued interest in their business and how you can help.

Now comes the real work. You see someone who you recognize from Linkedin. You approach him, introduce yourself while you shake hands, and begin a conversation. To avoid getting tongue tied, you soon use the conversation starter questions you had prepared. After ten minutes, you learn quite a bit about this individual, and you both commit to connecting after the event for a future meeting. (If it works for both of you, perhaps you schedule the meeting on the spot.)

Over the next hour and a half, you make three additional positive connections with people you didn't previously know. You also meet several other folks who may not be good business connections, but they are enjoyable to speak to, nonetheless.

The next day, you review the business cards you received and determine where the potential business is. You immediately send an email to let each of these new contacts know that you enjoyed meeting them at the event and offer a few dates for a follow-up meeting or phone call with them. One woman said she was very interested in your services now, so you let her know in the email that you will call her later that day at a specific time.

Two of the people seem like very good prospects, so you want to make them feel special. In addition to the email, you also send them a simple handwritten note, if possible, referencing something from your conversation at the event. You put those notes in the mailbox during lunch. And later you call the woman with the pressing business need. (When you do meet with your new prospects, you make sure you are prepared, so as not to waste anybody's time — especially your own.)

Within 24 hours, you input the new prospects into your database, usually called a CRM (Customer Relationship Management system). You schedule alerts to remind yourself to keep in touch with the new prospects via email, phone calls, and handwritten notes until they become a client.

In a nutshell, being intentional is the key to the work required to making networking fruitful. Be intentional about preparing for the event. Be intentional about meeting people at the event. Be intentional about following up after the event. And be very intentional to not let the connection die after your first meeting.

Believe me. It certainly makes all your hard work worth it when you change a person's designation in your CRM from Prospect to Client!

Notes

_____

_____

_____

_____

_____

_____

_____

_____

_____

_____

_____

_____

_____

_____

_____

_____

_____

_____

Notes

_____

_____

_____

_____

_____

_____

_____

_____

_____

_____

_____

_____

_____

_____

_____

_____

Chapter Twenty One

Stuck in Ruts, Traps and Friendships

I often hear from people that they find themselves feeling stuck when it comes to their networking efforts. Feeling like they're meeting the same people at the same events. I know exactly how that feels. Sometimes I have gotten frustrated and I'd stop going to specific networking events because I felt like I was spinning my wheels. (In truth, I was probably just being lazy.) I would get into a rut, going to the same events repeatedly. Speaking to the same people. Or connecting with people that I know won't benefit my business but are easy to talk to. They may have different faces, but at the end of the day, they're the same as the person I met last time.

And to make matters worse, they aren't even my ideal target client. But that is not their fault; it's my fault. I must invest the time to find events that can be more fruitful for my business. I must invest the time to find places and events where my target clients and best referral sources will be in attendance. There's an old saying: If you keep doing what you've been doing, then you'll keep getting what you've got.

Or even worse, the saying that insanity is defined as doing the same thing over and over, expecting different results. If that is the definition of insanity, then there are a lot of insane people at networking events.

Therefore, from time to time, even I must go back to basics. People often call me the expert networker, especially since I wrote a book on the subject, "Intentional Networking". But I must remind these people that even I still have a lot to learn. I still drop the ball from time to time. For example, I sometimes forget to follow up with a prospect. That is why, from time to time, I review what is working, what is not working, and what I can do differently.

One thing I might do is "play some oldies." There are certain networking events and groups that I used to go to regularly, but then for various reasons, they were no longer fruitful, and so I stopped going. I have recently started going back to some of those groups after a couple of years of having been away from them. Outside of a couple familiar faces, almost everybody else is new. It really freshens things up! Interestingly, I had gotten several speaking engagements and many new coaching clients just from attending networking groups that I had stopped visiting at one time and revisited after a period of time away.

Of course, I must be very careful when I go back to these groups not to fall into the friend trap. We all know that trap so well. You don't? Oh, well let me tell you…

You know that sense of terror? The one that grips you when you enter a room full of strangers, where you plan to meet many of them to grow your business? It often comes with that pit in your stomach. Or a large dose of paralysis. Or both. We've all felt it.

Then, in an instant, it all changes, when you recognize somebody in the room. Immediately, without thinking, you go up to them and start talking. And now you're relaxed and comfortable. The large, cold, scary room is now warm, cozy and safe.

Beware! You've fallen into a trap – the Friend Trap! It seems like the right thing to do — speaking for 20 or 30 or 60 minutes to one or two friends. But it's not! In fact, it's the opposite. You're killing your networking and business development efforts! Run!

I remember a few years ago when I went to a networking breakfast where I almost got caught in the Friend Trap. I walked into the City Club of Raleigh. It is a beautiful establishment, on the 28th floor of a downtown office building. The windows everywhere offer incredible views of Raleigh and miles of the beautiful North Carolina landscape.

That day, there were around fifty people there that I did not know. Fifty different reasons for me to have a panic attack. Luckily, when I arrived, I saw my friend Marie. I immediately went over, said hello, and we began to catch up. Aahhhh…safety. Then another friend, Marc, walked in and immediately made his way over to us. He was safe now as well. There we were. A small group. A clique. In a warm, safe place.

Interestingly, neither Marie nor Marc has ever given me a referral. And based on my memory at that time, I was sure I had never given either of them a referral either. So why in the world were we standing there speaking to each other in a room full of new business opportunities? BECAUSE IT WAS SAFE!!!

After two or three minutes, my inner relationship marketing coach yelled, "RUN, JOE! RUN! YOU'RE IN THE FRIEND TRAP!"

I then said to Marie and Marc, "I am not following my own rule by standing here talking to my friends. I'm going to go meet new people." They both agreed, and the three of us walked off in separate directions. In the next thirty minutes, I met and spoke with four wonderful people. Two of those new people were very good connections who each turned into new business.

The next time you are at a business event, beware the Friend Trap! If you find yourself caught in the Friend Trap, pretend you are in a B horror movie, where the audience is screaming at you from their seats, "RUN! GET OUT OF THE FRIEND TRAP!"

When you do find your networking in a rut, review what you're doing. What's working? What's not working? What are you doing that you can be doing differently? Then make the necessary adjustments. They're probably much easier to make than you think. At least I have found it to be so.

What 3 to 5 bad habits can you stop doing when networking that are currently hurting your efforts?

01.

02.

03.

04.

05.

What 3 to 5 new habits can you implement when networking that will improve your efforts? *(And then of course start doing them.)*

01.

02.

03.

04.

05.

Notes

_____

_____

_____

_____

_____

_____

_____

_____

_____

_____

_____

_____

_____

_____

_____

_____

PART FOUR

Mindset Is an Inside Job

JOSEPH NOVARA

Chapter Twenty Two

The Rabbit Hole and a Joyful Return

I go to church most Sundays. I love the church I attend. The pastor always gives a powerful message, and the worship band is made up of some extremely talented musicians. I remember one particular worship service, the band was jamming quite powerfully. I felt great and was singing at the top of my lungs. Yep, I was that guy. I felt hopeful. Alive.

Then something happened.

For some reason my mind began to wander. As I was singing the next couple of songs, I began to think about the failures in my life over the past few years. I slipped deeper and deeper into a dark place. Just ten minutes before I was full of hope, and now I was lost, hopeless, and ready to give up. I no longer felt great.

Then it hit me. I had to put a stop to this – and immediately. I decided at that moment that I was not going to feel those feelings of hopelessness and dejection. I didn't know where they came from or why I was suddenly feeling them, but I refused to give them any more power over me.

The first thing I did was change my thinking back to positive, hopeful thoughts. When my mind tried to wander back to the negative place, I said, "Nope! We're not going there!" Instead, I focused on positive, upbeat things. That church service turned out to be one of the best I had ever been to.

Later that day, I took some time to reflect on my short breakdown earlier. Why had that happened? Why had I gone into that dark spiral? After some quiet time alone, I figured it out. From my seat at church, I was trying to fix the mistakes and failures of my recent past. I had gone down the "what ifs" rabbit hole. That hole goes nowhere. There is no end to the rabbit hole of "what ifs." It lures you in deeper and deeper, where it gets darker and darker. Where it gets more painful. Further from reality.

That wasn't my first time down one of those rabbit holes. There were times in my past where I had gone so deep that it led to days, weeks or even months of resentment, anger, and depression. However, I have successfully worked for years on improving my mind that I generally catch myself before I reach a point of pain that will take a long time to recover from. I don't like pain. I don't like negativity. I choose not to live there, and I choose not to have negative people in my inner circle. I spend the majority of my time with positive, encouraging people. Men and women who work hard, love life, and welcome abundance into their lives. My inner self avoids the Debbie Downers and Negative Normans of the world. If someone wants to live in deprivation, whether emotionally, spiritually or financially, then so be it, but I will move on. I need to be around victors, not victims.

We all have the ability to make the same choice I made that Sunday. Don't question it. Just make it. Choose positive thoughts and hope. Choose joy!

Notes

_____

_____

_____

_____

_____

_____

_____

_____

_____

_____

_____

_____

_____

_____

_____

_____

_____

_____

Chapter Twenty Three
The Knuckleheads Guide
to Goal Setting

It was the summer of 1996. I lived in Brooklyn, NY at that time. My on again off again girlfriend Jackie and I were talking about taking our relationship to the next level. Co-habitation. She and I had never even taken a vacation together and here we were, talking about moving in together. I suggested we go on vacation. Something easy. Not too far. We decided on visiting Niagara Falls, figuring we would stay in Buffalo which is right outside of Niagara, NY.

I didn't call ahead to reserve a room; however, this is Buffalo, NY we're talking about. We will have no problem finding a hotel room. I looked at a road map my friend owned and wrote down the roads I believed would get us up to Buffalo. Based on the course I mapped out, it should take us at most nine hours including a couple of rest stops along the way.

The big day arrived. Jackie and I loaded up the car and began our journey north. Once we were out of New York City, trouble started. One of the roads I had written down from the map was closed. After a few wrong turns and a couple of stops later to ask for directions, we were back on the right course. And still, the

131

directions I had written down were not as well written as I originally thought.

Jackie and I began snapping at each other. She was mad at me for not having written down better directions or had at least brought the map with us. I was frustrated with her based on her music choices on the radio. We bickered, followed by periods of giving each other the silent treatment. The once manageable nine hour drive now turned into a long, exhaustive fifteen hour drive.

When we arrived in Buffalo, we were drained, mentally and emotionally. But there was a light at the end of the tunnel. Maybe a good night's sleep would help us to feel better. We stopped at the first hotel we saw. They were fully booked with no rooms available. We drove to another hotel right next door, but we experienced the same problem. Fully booked.

We then drove from one hotel to another. We even stopped at the seediest motels. Anything that looked like an overnight establishment. Everything was booked. What we hadn't known was we had picked a weekend to visit when there were two business conferences and an airshow happening in Buffalo, all at the same time.

We began making phone calls to other hotels and motels in Buffalo and the surrounding areas on the United States side. We couldn't find a room within a sixty mile radius on the U.S. side. We ended up driving seventy five miles to Rochester, NY to stay at a very overpriced Hilton.

Needless to say, Jackie and I never did take our relationship to the next level. After a couple of days, we decided to cut the trip short. We also decided to call an end to our blooming relationship.

That was the last time I ever took a vacation without planning ahead, such as getting proper directions, booking a room well in advance and even having some activities planned.

I'm guessing you may be asking yourself at this point, "What in the world does this have anything to do with setting goals?" I'm glad you asked, and I'm now going to tell you.

For a very long time, I treated my goals exactly the same way I treated what was supposed to be a "life changing" vacation. I would set goals. Big goals. But there would be no plan to go along with these goals. I would proclaim on January 1 of each year a list of goals I hoped to accomplish without having any idea how I was going to accomplish them.

I started to get sick of hearing myself say "my goal is to do this", or "my goal is to do that". Whenever I would say "My goal is_____" I began to cringe. I realized that all my goals were just dreams. Dreams that were already unfulfilled or destined for obscurity. Nothing more. Then one day it occurred to me that I was treating my goals just like I had treated the trip with Jackie. No plans. No direction. No true destination. I remembered my commitment to never let that happen again with one of my trips.

I thought to myself, what if I start treating my goals the same way I eventually learned to plan my road trips. Isn't a goal just a destination? A place we are working to get to. So, I began to write down my goals. Once I had a starting point and an end point, then I had to fill in the directions to get there. The plan.

Of course, depending on the size of the goal, some were more difficult than others. The planning process for some goals was very simple and I could knock it out on my own. Some goals were much bigger and required the help of friends, mentors and coaches. In some cases, the goal you are shooting for may be big enough that there may be a need to call in paid help. If the return on investment is worth the cost to reach your goal, then don't be afraid to make a financial investment.

I have found having a plan attached to a goal creates confidence and clarity. My friend Dori Staehle taught me once that in sales…

Confidence and Clarity equals Clients and Cash.

So please remember, A goal without a plan is just a wish. And that is okay. There is nothing wrong with wishes, however, it is important not to confuse the two. Earl Nightengale said, "People with goals succeed because they know where they're going." Plan out your goals and you will undoubtedly be a success.

Name Specific Goal...

_____

_____

Why this particular goal?

_____

_____

Time Frame to accomplish your goal? (Time/Date)

_____

Who is your accountability partner/team for your goal?

_____

_____

What 3 to 6 action items are required to accomplish
your specific goal?

     01. _____

     02. _____

     03. _____

     04. _____

     05. _____

     06. _____

Notes

Chapter Twenty Four

The Giver

As a person running a business, having the mindset of, take, take, take is a very easy trap to fall into. You have bills to pay. Kids to feed. Pets to groom. Vacations to pay for. Car payments. A mortgage or rent. Maybe employees to pay. Different insurances, and the list goes on ad nauseum.

How can someone be expected to have a givers mindset when all of this weighs so heavily on the mind of many small business owners today? Building relationships is the furthest thing from many business owners minds, unless the relationship is one where a client is going to purchase, over and over again.

That creates the question of, "How do I create that kind of relationship and yet, still have a spirit of giving that allows me to focus on others and not only my needs?" The answer is simple. It takes time. And, you must be very intentional about it.

My friend Durwood Lassiter is a sales representative for a large printing company in North Carolina, named Joseph C. Woodard Printing. Durwood truly has the spirit of giving. He has been in the printing industry for over thirty years. Technically, he could sit back now and just ride the incoming wave of residual income from previous clients.

To that point, the printing industry is also very aggressive, so there are always other local printing companies coming after his clients. And, the online discount printers are marketing heavily to his clients through social media ads and pop up banners. This could create much anxiety in any sales representative.

Instead, Durwood is constantly looking for ways that he can give back to his community, his clients and even prospects. He invests his time in two non-profits that he started with his wife. One focused on helping adults with leukemia and the other helping bring awareness to Domestic Violence. On top of that, he also volunteers to help create events to honor purple heart heroes around the state of North Carolina.

Honestly, he is very humble about it all. He and I have been friends for several years and he never brags about it. I can remember when he was doing fundraisers, which I thought he had gotten pulled into helping someone else. I couldn't have been more wrong. He is all about giving back. His mindset is, "What can I do to help others in and around my community to live a better life?"

What's important is having the mindset of, "What can I do to help others?" I am not saying you should ever put yourself in a dangerous position where you are not bringing in an income for yourself while making the lives of others better. What I am saying is that along with growing your client base: along with filling your sales funnel: along with growing your bottom line, you must find ways to give with no expectation of anything in return. The rewards present themselves without you even looking.

I like to consider myself a giver. I love to connect people in business. I love to encourage people when they need encouraging. I love to lend a hand when someone has a need. My mind is free. I feel loved because I offer love. Yes, you can offer love in business. You show it by your actions.

Because of who I am, I have had people help me during times of personal crisis in ways that I would have never imagined possible. During my divorce, I had friends that had once started as business relationships, support me emotionally when I felt I was at the end of my rope. I've had friends that had once begun as business relationships help me paint my house when I was selling it. I've had business friends offer to help me move, and then show up to actually do it. I've had friends cover enormous down payments to allow a business transaction to go through, with no reward for them at the other end, aside from getting repaid.

This also shows up in business as well. As a giver, people will show up to refer you or your business when they hear of a need that you can fill. You will likely be the first person they think of. As a person known to the business community as a giver, your name is most often the only one people will think of.

If you work in a more a corporate environment, this is still just as easy. Volunteer in committees that will improve the well-being of other employees. Be a part of the health and wellness program. If there isn't one, talk to human resources to find out how you can start one. Get to know as many people within your organization as you possible can. Always share a smile. Always have a kind word. Learn about your fellow employees. And look for opportunities to give. The company you work for can be your community.

When we give selflessly, it helps to improve our self-esteem, we experience improved confidence, we feel happier, we enjoy life a little more and people take notice. Find a cause that you are passionate about. Something you enjoy being a part of. Something that won't feel like a burden, but instead will feel life giving and then get involved. Today!

Find a person who needs encouraging. Find a business or a salesperson that could use a referral. Find some way that you can make a positive impact in someone else's life and do it. Today!

Notes

_____

_____

_____

_____

_____

_____

_____

_____

_____

_____

_____

_____

_____

_____

_____

_____

_____

_____

Notes

Conclusion

I am so grateful for the people in my life. When I first began writing this book, I had a different vision of what the final product would look like. Along the way, God changed my vision and I went with His. He put people in my life that helped me to follow a different track and to discover new and improved ways of growing a business. He opened my eyes to see how I'd been doing things that were helping to grow my business but hadn't recognized as essential and important.

I practice what I preach and that is why I feel confident in sharing it with you within these pages. Relationships are extremely important to me, both in my personal life and in my professional life. I want to encourage you to do the same.

When the walls feel like they're coming down around you (if you're a business owner or sales professional, that will happen at least once in your career), and you feel like you're at the end of your rope, it is the relationships you develop that will help you through whatever circumstance you find yourself in.

"Grow Your Network, Grow Your Business" sounds so simple, yet everyday, business people struggle with getting this concept right. People want to grow their business first without putting in the leg work to grow and nurture their network first. Then they wonder why they can't seem to develop loyalty with their client base.

There are so many different ways we can prospect, market and grow our businesses. Go to sales and professional development seminars. Watch business and or inspirational videos on YouTube. Read books from the top experts in sales, marketing, social media, prospecting and professional development. Never stop learning. And never stop growing and nurturing your network.

Growth doesn't happen by accident. I am honored that you have taken the time to read my book. Now use it for everything it has. Write in it. Use the note pages to keep track of your progress. Utilize the forms. Print them out again and again to see how you're improving and changing.

Hire a coach. Engage a mentor. Join a mastermind group. You don't have to go through this journey alone. Even the Lone Ranger hung out with Tonto. Keep moving forward, and remember, Grow Your Network, Grow Your Business, and as a result, you will, without a doubt, increase your revenue.

Thank You!

Special Bonus From Joe

I am so happy you purchased this book. It shows that you are serious about Growing Your Network and Growing Your Business. I want to send you special bonus' that will help you on your way to intentional prospecting greatness.

To receive your special bonus', simply register here:

www.joenovara.com/GYNGYB-Goodies

All the forms from within this book as well as additional goodies will be available for you to download from the above link.

If you have any questions about Growing Your Network and Growing Your Business, email me at **joe@joenovara.com**.

Contact me at the same email address for availability for speaking, workshops and coaching.

Made in the USA
Columbia, SC
06 March 2020